GOD'S LOVE IS...

UNSTOP-PABLE

10 BIG SESSIONS

EXPLORING THE LIFE OF PETER

ACTIVITIES AND WORKSHEETS
BURSTING WITH FUN AND TRUTH

FOR USE WITH CHILDREN AGED 7-11

BIG
MINISTRIES

Copyright © 2013 BIG Ministries

First published in 2013 by Elevation
Elevation is part of Memralife Group, registered charity number 1126997,
a company limited by guarantee, registered in England and Wales,
number 6667924. 14 Horsted Square, Uckfield, East Sussex, TN22 1QG

British Library Cataloguing in Publication Data

A catalogue record for this book is available from the British Library

ISBN 978-1-899788-93-4

Cover Design: Dan Armstrong at Wildfire Studio and Steve Squires
Additional Illustration: Sarah Joy at Random Panda
Design: Steve Squires

Printed by Saxoprint

CONTENTS

The Blob Family

What's the BIG Idea?

The BIG Idea is to look at nine stories from Peter's life, and to use these stories as a foundation for each session, bringing out themes that are important and relevant to children in their journey with God. These are combined with songs from the BIG Ministries album *God's Love is Unstoppable* to help children really get to grips with the themes.

For nine sessions we are looking at foundational themes from the life of Peter, things he went through and what he learnt from those experiences. We will be using him as an example of a follower of Jesus.

The tenth session is a special super-fun session all about rhythm!

How to use this book

Although the sessions will work without the songs, we recommend you purchase a copy of *God's Love Is Unstoppable* to use alongside this book, as the songs are a key part. You can buy this from *www.bigministries.co.uk* or download the songs from *iTunes*.

Alongside the songs, each session includes craft ideas, games ideas, teaching material, and other fun activities. There are guideline timings with each activity along with checklists for all the things you'll need so that preparation is as simple as possible!

Each session can run for 45 minutes to an hour depending on how long you have.

There is a ready-to-go interactive Bible story in every session, as well as a photocopiable worksheet to do with the children.

The idea of the worksheet is that it is a foundation for discussion. Some children will want to do every little part of the sheet, some will possibly just do the puzzles(!). Either is fine, but the aim is to get the children talking about the issues while they're doing what they want to on the sheet. (There is a lot of fun things on each sheet so, if you're able, it may be worth copying them onto A3.)

Have fun hearing stories from Peter's life, worshipping God through some great songs and learning all about becoming a follower of Jesus.

FOLLOWING JESUS

C'MON EVERYBODY

PLAY IT · **You will need:**

4-6 mins

- Nothing! (Although you might find some background music helpful)

Play a game of 'I Can Do This'

Get the children standing in a circle. One at a time the children are to do something that all of the other children then have to copy. For example, one child says 'I can do this... can you?' and proceeds to pull a funny face. All of the other children then have to copy that child. It is then the next child's turn. The game can be as energetic or as relaxed as you wish.

(Alternatively you could lead a game of 'Simon Says'.)

NTRO IT · **You will need:**

6 mins

- At least 10 pictures of different people, on separate sheets of paper (the people should be well known such as the Queen or famous TV celebrities, and some generic professional people, such as policemen, doctors, chefs, builders. You could even include a picture of someone 'well known' from your church / club)

Lay out the pictures of the people and ask the children to put them in order of who they think is the most important, to the person that they think is the least important. If you have a large group you may need a few sets of pictures.

Ask the children about their reasons for the way that they've ordered the pictures.

Tell the children that the theme of the day is *Following Jesus*.

Tell the children this:
We tend to see some people as more important than other people, often because of the things that they do. God sees people differently to how we see them. In His eyes, everyone is just as important as the next person. He calls everyone to follow Him.

TELL IT · **You will need:**

7 mins

- Story script (starting on page 12)

Teach the children the trigger words and encourage them to interact as you tell them the story.

You will need:

- *God's Love Is Unstoppable* album and the facilities to play it

Sing *C'mon Everybody* together (Track 2).

Song actions can be found at www.bigministries.co.uk.

You will need:

- An activity sheet copied for each child (on page 14)
- Pens/pencils
- Bibles

Go through the sheet - use it as a foundation for discussion. Allow the children to do the sheet however they would like to, but talk to them about the key questions as they are doing things.

Option 1 - **Celebration bunting!**

You will need:

- Lots of large diamond shaped pieces of paper (when folded it becomes an isosceles triangle)
- Glue
- Colouring pens
- String
- Decorative foam shapes, stickers and sequins

1. First, give each child one or two diamonds and ask them to get their decoration skills going!

2. When they have finished decorating, get the children to attach their diamonds by folding them (decorated side on the outside) over the string and glueing them together.

3. Hey presto! You have created some awesome bunting!

Option 2 - **A fishing net**

You will need:

- A wire coat-hanger for each child
- Mesh netting - cut into circles of approx. 4ft diameter.
- Scissors
- Strong tape, (gaffer tape is ideal)
- Long shoe lace, for each child
- Wooden stick, 2 feet long, for each child (bamboo sticks are perfect)

1. Bend the triangular part of the hanger into a smooth circle shape.

2. Straighten the hook part of the hanger.

3. Give each child a circle of mesh.

4. Wrap the circumference of the mesh netting around the wire hanger and use the tape to secure it in place.

5. Weave a shoe lace in and out of the circumference of the mesh netting and over the wire hanger to make perfectly sure that the net will not fall off.

6. Lay the straightened hook of the hanger along the wooden stick, and secure it with the tape.

7. Voilà! A fishing net!

 You will need:

3 mins

- A large piece of paper with the words 'Follower of Jesus' written in the middle
- A few plates with different coloured paint on
- Wet wipes
- Pens

Ask the children to think about whether or not they'd like to be a follower of Jesus and, if they would like to, to commit to following Him by placing one of their fingers in some paint and printing their fingerprint on the large piece of paper.

They could write a prayer next to their print too.

JESUS CALLS THE FIRST DISCIPLES

(Luke 5:1-11)

TRIGGER WORDS   **Fishermen:** "1, 2, 3, 4, 5, once I caught a fish alive!"
Absolutely nothing: "Not one fish!"
Following/Follow/Followed: "Wait for me!"

Peter and his brother Andrew were **fishermen**. All night they had been out on the lake in their boat doing their job, and all night, while they were out on the lake, they had caught **absolutely nothing**! Not one fish.

"Grrr. Is there not even one fish in this lake?" Peter groaned. "Looks like were going back to shore with nothing! **Absolutely nothing**! Not one fish."

And so back to shore they went, tired from a long night and disappointed with catching **absolutely nothing**! Not even one fish. Peter and his brother Andrew collected their nets and hauled them onto dry land. As they began fixing holes and clearing seaweed and dirt from the nets, they looked a short way along the beach and noticed a large gathering of people making their way nearer.

"Peter, what have you done now?" said Andrew to his brother, expecting him to have offended some of the locals.

"Me? Nothing! Why are you always accusing me?" responded Peter in a fairly surprised tone, as if he didn't know what his brother was on about.

As the people made their way nearer it was clear that they were all **following** one man in particular. Someone that must have caught their attention in one way or another. Someone who must have been worth listening to. Someone who must have been worth **following**. The man's name was Jesus.

"They're still coming this way Peter. Are you sure you haven't done anything to upset anyone?"

"Give it a rest!" responded Peter to his brother, who was only trying to wind him up.

The two **fishermen** continued cleaning their nets as the crowd gathered nearer and nearer, **following** Jesus. Jesus then approached Peter and said to him, "Do you mind if I talk to the crowd from your boat?"

And so, Peter and his brother Andrew, got in the boat with Jesus and pushed out a little from shore so He could talk to the people.

When Jesus was done, He then said to Peter, "Let's go out a bit further into the lake and let down the nets to catch some fish."

Now, if you recall, Peter and Andrew had been out fishing all night and had caught **absolutely nothing**! Not one fish!

"We've worked hard all night," said Peter, "and we've caught **absolutely nothing**! Not one fish! But because you say so, we'll do it."

And so they sailed out into deep water. They took hold of the nets and cast them over the edge of the boat. Only a matter of seconds later, the net started moving, and the boat started swaying and rocking. Fish were gathering in the nets like no other time before. In fact, so many fish gathered in the nets that the nets began to stretch and break.

Nearby was another boat with two other **fishermen**. Their names were James and John.

"James! John!" shouted Peter. "Get over here and help us would you!?"

Both boats then loaded the immense catch of fish onto their deck. They had never seen so many fish. The boats were so heavy with fish that they began to sink.

Peter was frozen in sheer amazement with what had just happened and, falling to his knees in front of Jesus, he then said, "Leave me alone Lord, I am a sinful man."

Jesus just looked at Peter and calmly said these words, "Don't be afraid. **Follow** me. From now on you will fish for people."

And that was that. The **fishermen**—Peter, his brother Andrew, and James and John—left their boats and their nets and everything else they owned, and immediately **followed** Jesus.

FOLLOWING JESUS

NAME

Come on everybody...
It's time to start this party!

He said **WHAT**?!

Jesus said, "From now on, you'll fish for people."

What?

What was Peter thinking...

... when the net was full of fish?

BIG STORY

Peter & Andrew had been fishing **all night**, and caught **nothing**. Jesus came into their boat to talk to a crowd of people.

He told them to put their net back into the water and they caught **loads of fish!** Jesus then asked Peter & Andrew to **follow him!**

Luke 5: 1-11

Draw a cool fish here...

All is not as it seems... Peter & Andrew leaving everything and following Jesus was even more exciting than it seemed! So – time for a bit of history! **Trust me...** it's cool history!

When Jesus was on Earth, all Jewish boys aged 6 went to **TORAH SCHOOL!**

The **Torah** is what Jews call the first 5 books of the Bible. Do you know what they are?

1. G.............
2. E.............
3. L.............
4. N.............
5. D.............

In Jesus' time, only boys went to school...

Let's meet three TORAH SCHOOL students!

HI, I'M JOHNNY

HI, I'M FREDDY

HI, I'M TOMMY

	Age 6	Age 10	Age 14
JOHNNY	MEMORISE (yes, learn!) the Torah and take EXAMS	FAILED	Learns to do what Dad does... like be a **fisherman!**
FREDDY		GOT A	Applies to follow a Rabbi* Rabbi says **"NO** – you're not good enough". Woe is me!
TOMMY		GOT A	Applies to follow a Rabbi... Rabbi says **"YES!** Come follow me!" Yippeee!

NOT A DISCIPLE

NOT A DISCIPLE

This only happens if you're the **BEST** student **AND** the Rabbi thinks you're good enough!

"DISCIPLE"
(Being like your Rabbi)

TORAH SCHOOL

* Psst... A **Rabbi** was a teacher that people followed around.

Peter & Andrew were fishermen. This means they weren't good enough to stay at **TORAH SCHOOL** or follow a Rabbi! They'd **FAILED**. BUT Jesus calls them to follow him – **even though** they hadn't passed all the tests! Jesus believed they could be like him! **AND** he thinks that about us too!

CHECK IT OUT!
Matthew 18: 20

How can we follow Jesus today?
We can't...

PRAY!

Thank Jesus for asking us to follow him. **Ask him** to help you **follow him well!**

PUZZLE CORNER

IT'S AGAINST THE CLOCK!
You've got **1 MINUTE!**

Can you "follow Jesus" to the lake?

LAKE

TOTAL WIPEOUT

Big MINISTRIES

PRAYING

THANK YOU FOR LISTENING

 PLAY IT

5 mins

You will need:

- A list of generic questions that can be asked to any child
- A buzzer or a bell
- Some prizes

Play the 'Yes, No' game

One child has the question sheet and asks another child a series of questions to which they can reply with anything but the words, 'yes' or 'no'.

Have another person with the buzzer, ready to buzz whenever 'yes' or 'no' is said!

Invite the children to take it in turns to be 'interviewed'. Give every child a prize after their go.

 INTRO IT

4 mins

You will need:

- A piece of paper for each child
- A pen or pencil for each child

Tell the children that the theme of the day is *Prayer*.

Ask the children what they think prayer is.

Give each child a piece of paper and a pen.

Tell them to all be really quiet and write down as many sounds as they can hear. (If they listen really hard they should be able to hear sounds that they hadn't noticed were there.)

Allow the children to share what they've written.

Talk to the children about prayer not just being about talking, but that sometimes we need to listen to God too.

Read this passage from 1 Kings 19:11-12:

'Then he (Elijah) was told, "Go, stand on the mountain at attention before God. God will pass by." A hurricane wind ripped through the mountains and shattered the rocks before God, but God wasn't to be found in the wind; after the wind an earthquake, but God wasn't in the earthquake; and after the earthquake, fire, but God wasn't in the fire; and after the fire, a gentle and quiet whisper.'

God was in the quiet whisper... we need to make sure we are listening for Him!

TELL IT

You will need:

- Story script (starting on page 18)

Teach the children the trigger words and encourage them to interact as you tell them the story.

7 mins

 SING IT

You will need:

- *God's Love Is Unstoppable* album and facilities to play it

Sing *Thank You For Listening* together (Track 3).

Song actions can be found at *www.bigministries.co.uk*.

5 mins

 TALK ABOUT IT

You will need:

- An activity sheet copied for each child (on page 20)
- Pens/pencils
- Bibles

Go through the worksheet. Use it as a foundation for discussion. Allow the children to do the sheet however they would like to, but talk to them about the key questions as they are doing things.

10-13 mins

 CREATE IT

You will need:

- Each child will need - three corks, two cocktail sticks and two lolly sticks
- Sheets of foam
- Scissors
- Strong glue (hot glue gun if you have one)
- String

10 mins

We are going to make a boat (that will hopefully float!).

The three corks make the base for the boat. Lay them down parallel to each other about 1.5cm apart. (One lolly stick should span the total width of the three corks.) Use the two lolly sticks to make the top for the boat by sticking them flat on top of the three corks (see below). [If you're not sure about this, drop us an email and we'll try to help! *info@bigministries.co.uk*.]

Cut three squares of foam, fold them loosely in half and pierce them top and bottom with the cocktail stick - these will be your sails. Stick a cocktail stick sail in each cork.

You can use string for additional security of the lolly sticks, and for making a tow line if you'd like!

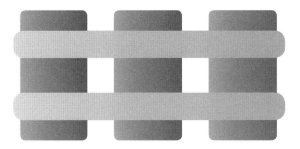

You will need:

- A flower template made from sugar-paper for each child (using the below image as a model)
- Scissors
- Pens
- Tray with water in

Invite the children to write / draw prayers on their flowers.

Cut the flowers out and fold over the petals to conceal the prayer.

Float the flower prayers on the water and slowly they will open up, symbolising offering the prayers to God.

JESUS CALMS THE STORM
(Matthew 8:23-27; Mark 4:35-41; Luke 8:22-25)

TRIGGER WORDS
Boat: 'Ahoy there!'
Sleeping: Snore.
Waves/wave: Make the noise of a wave crashing.
Thunder: Clap your hands together once.
Wind: Make the noise of a strong wind.
Rain: On the floor, or on a hard surface, tap your fingers to make the sound of pitter-pattering rain.

The disciples were all in a **boat**; twelve disciples in total - Peter, his brother Andrew, James, John, Philip, Bartholomew, Matthew, Thomas, James son of Alphaeus, Simon, Judas son of James, and Judas Iscariot; all of them sailing in a **boat** across to the opposite side of Lake Galilee. And of course, Jesus was with them. Although at this precise moment in time, He was **sleeping**.

Splish, splash, splosh went the **boat** as it bobbed up and down, gliding its way through the waters. Splish splash splosh went the **boat** as tiny ripples and **waves** collided in its path.

"Yawn," Peter yawned, "I think Jesus has got the right idea," and he stretched out his arms preparing himself to get comfy for a little snooze of his own.

Splish, splash, splosh went the **boat** as it bobbed up and down, gliding its way through the waters. Splish, splash, splosh went the **boat** as tiny ripples and **waves** collided in its path. Splish, splash, SPLASH! A slightly larger **wave** took the disciples by surprise, soaking Peter just as he was about to lie down.

"Oh! Now I'm all wet!" said Peter trying to dry himself with Andrew's clothes.

All that the other disciples could do was laugh at Peter's misfortune...

"Ha ha ha ha!"

They laughed until... Splish, SPLASH, SPLASH! Another two **waves**, larger than the previous, shook the **boat** and completely drenched them all.

"That'll stop your laughing," Peter said, feeling rather smug.

But that wasn't to be the only thing that would stop the disciples laughing. For in the distance, heading straight towards them, was the thickest, darkest, cloudiest cloud that they ever did see. Forks of lightning could be seen flashing in the distance, rumbles of **thunder** could be heard, and the **wind** began to grow stronger and heavier, pushing the **boat** forwards and backwards, and from side to side. It was enough to make anyone feel sick.

Splish, SPLASH, SPLASH, SPLASH, WHOOSH!

A gigantic **wave** crashed onto the **boat**, knocking the disciples to the floor.

"I think we're in trouble here," said one of the disciples in a slight panic.

The **wind** grew stronger, the **waves** grew bigger, the **rain** grew heavier and the **thunder** grew louder. Soon enough the twelve disciples were in the middle of one of the most ferocious storms that they'd ever encountered. They feared for their lives and gripped hold of whatever they could find to grip hold of. Then, they all screamed.

"ARRRRRRRRRRRGGHH!"

And still the **wind** grew stronger, the **waves** grew bigger, the **rain** grew heavier and the **thunder** grew louder. Whatever were they to do? There was no way they could battle against this storm. It was just too strong.

Now, you may be asking what Jesus was doing in all of this commotion. Well, let me tell you— He was **sleeping**. Jesus was still **sleeping**. Through all of the splishing, sploshing, splashing and whooshing; the **wind**, the **waves**, the **rain**, the **thunder**, the lightning, as well as the rocking side to side and back and forth, Jesus still remained **sleeping**.

It was at the point when the disciples were certain that their time had come—meaning, they thought they were going to die—that they had a great idea...

"Jesus! WAKE UP! WAKE UP! WAKE UP! We're going to drown in this storm!" they all shouted, gripping Him by His clothes and shaking Him desperately.

Jesus lifted Himself to his feet and spoke out in a strong and stern voice, "**Wind, waves, rain, thunder**, be still."

And did the **wind** and **waves** and **rain** and **thunder** continue? Of course not. Jesus had spoken and the weather obeyed His words. The storm was over and the waters grew calm.

"Where is your faith?" Jesus asked the disciples.

The disciples remained gripping onto the edge of the **boat**, dripping with water and utterly overwhelmed by what had just happened. Then they began speaking amongst themselves saying, "Who is this? He can even command the weather."

And with that, they continued on their journey to the other side of the lake, with only a gentle splish, splash, splosh as the **boat** bobbed up and down, gliding its way, very peacefully, through the waters.

PRAYING

8

NAME

BIG STORY

Peter and the disciples were out in the boat. Jesus was with them, but asleep in the boat. A **massive storm** arrived.

The disciples were scared and woke Jesus up. He told the storm to **"Be Still"** – and it was! **AMAZING!**

Mark 4: 35–41

PUZZLE CORNER...

IT'S AGAINST THE CLOCK!

You've got **1 MINUTE!**

How many **fish** can you draw in this **net**? Ready, steady... **GO!**

PSST... They only count if they actually look like fish! <><

Do we have to wake Jesus up before we can speak to him?

Have you ever been **outside in a massive storm**?

How did you feel?

CHECK IT OUT!
Ephesians 6: 18

What was Peter thinking... ... during the storm?

It's so good to know that wherever we are, whatever we're doing, **we can talk to Jesus** and know he's listening (and he's good at answering prayers too... and he understands what we're going through!).

It's a total mystery, that I speak and you hear me. You respond amazingly with what I really need...

Jesus is **POWERFUL** (he did all the creating!). Do you know the story of Jesus calming the storm? *(If not, you can look it up – Mark 4:35-41).*

Can you tell the story in **3** pictures?

Just with his words, Jesus stopped a storm...

We have Jesus with us still today – he's still that powerful. Think of all the amazing stuff he can do with us!

WOW!

He said WHAT?!

"Where is your faith?" Jesus said.

(But they woke him up... Isn't that having faith?)

Write or draw in the bubble letters things you want God's help with.

HELP

PRAY!

Thank Jesus that he's **always listening.** Then ask him **whatever you like!**

AMEN!

TRUSTING GOD

F.R.O.G.

5-8 mins

PLAY IT

You will need:

- A newspaper
- Party music and facilities to play it

Play a game of 'Musical Islands':

Spread out individual pages of newspaper across the floor - make sure there is enough for everyone to stand on.

Play some music and when the music stops, everyone must be standing on a piece of paper. Each time the music starts, take away more and more of the paper so that there is less to stand on. If anyone is not standing on some paper when the music stops, they are out and must stand at the side.

NB. You are allowed to share islands (if you can balance!).

6 mins

INTRO IT

You will need:

- Some sweets
- Blindfolds

Send a couple of people out of the room and while they are out of the room get them blindfolded. (Make sure they can't hear or see what is going on.)

Explain to the remaining children that you are going to offer the blindfolded children some sweets (or something that you know that the blindfolded children like and don't have allergies to!) when they re-enter the room.

Tell the children that they are to act repulsed by the sweets that the blindfolded children are about to eat, as if it's something really horrible.

Call the blindfolded children back into the room and ask them to trust you, that what you are going to feed them is good (without telling them what it is)... Encourage the other children in their 'repulsion' and see if the blindfolded children will let you place the sweets in their mouths... calmly keep telling them they can trust you!

When you've finished, make sure everyone gets a sweet and tell the children that the theme of the day is *Trusting God*.

Ask the children what they think it means to trust God. Talk to the children about the fact that sometimes trusting God can be difficult, especially when we don't know what's going to happen. However, trusting God is always the best thing to do, just like the people who, hopefully, trusted you and got the sweets!

You will need:

- Story script (starting on page 24)
- Dressing-up clothes / junk / action figures / play-dough / anything that you can think of that could be used to create different scenes in the story of *Walking on Water*

Divide the children into groups (or keep them altogether if it's a small group). Tell them that there will be certain points in the story where they are to create a 'still scene' (like a photo) depicting the part of the story they have just heard. They will use whatever materials you give them to do this.

Give them a time limit for each 'scene'. You could even make it a competition and award points, and perhaps take photos of each scene too, that you could use at a later date.

 You will need:

- *God's Love Is Unstoppable* album and facilities to play it

Sing *F.R.O.G.* together (Track 10).

Song actions can be found at *www.bigministries.co.uk*.

 You will need:

- An activity sheet copied for each child (on page 26)
- Pens/pencils
- Bibles

Go through the sheet using it as a foundation for discussion. Allow the children to do the sheet however they would like to, but talk to them about the key questions as they are doing things.

 You will need:

- Goggly eyes
- Card with a size ratio of 2:3 (business card sized works well, but is fiddly)
- Small stickers

Learn how to make a jumping frog! Go to: *http://blog.origamipapermonster.com* and search for jumping frog in the search bar. This will tell you everything you need to know!

Lead the children through making their frog.

Next, invite them to decorate their frog with stickers and goggly eyes for extra personality!

You will need:

- A large watertight container (preferably transparent)
- Water
- Permanent pens
- Selection of different weighted items (if you have no outside space)
- Some items that float that you are happy to give away (corks / feathers etc)

If possible, go outside with the children and get them to find a load of different objects. (If this is not possible, bring a large selection of things with you.)

Get the children to try and 'float' the objects and see which items sink.

Keep the things that 'float' separate.

Make sure every child has an object that floats and get them to write 'TRUST GOD' on it as a reminder about the story today and that we can trust God.

WALKING ON WATER

(Matthew 14:22-33)

Jesus had just fed over 5,000 people with five loaves of bread and two fish. There were still so many people who wanted to speak with Him and learn from Him, so Jesus sent the 12 disciples on ahead of Him.

"Get in the boat and go ahead of me to the other side of the lake," Jesus told them.

And so, they did just that. Climbing back into their boat and sailing out into the water there was only one thing that the disciples were talking about...

"...five loaves, two fish. I saw them with my own eyes," said one of the disciples, "How were all of those people fed?"

"More to the point", said another, "how were there 12 baskets left over at the end?" And so, the discussion went on.

[Scene 1: Five loaves and two fish]

The disciples, even after quite a while in the boat, hadn't managed to travel very far on the lake due to a strong wind blowing in the opposite direction to where they were headed.

Meanwhile, after Jesus had sent the crowds of people away, He went up on a mountainside to pray on His own.

[Scene 2: Jesus praying up a mountain]

Later on that evening, Jesus went out to meet the disciples who were still on the lake in their boat. But Jesus didn't go to meet them in another boat, nor did He swim. Jesus walked. That's right, He walked. Jesus set foot on the lake and walked on the surface of the water out to where the disciples were in their boat.

[Scene 3: The disciples in their boat, Jesus walking water]

Soon enough, the disciples stopped their chatting as they caught a glimpse of Jesus on the water...

"What is that!?" they asked, looking at one another.

"It's, it's, it's... a ghost!" said one of the disciples, sending everyone into a panicked frenzy.

"ARRRRRRGHHH!" The disciples screamed and tried to hide from the figure that they could see in the distance, not knowing who it was.

[Scene 4: The disciples looking panicked at the thought of seeing a ghost on the water]

But, to put them at ease, Jesus spoke out to them saying,

"Don't be afraid. It's me. Jesus."

Still feeling fairly confused by it all, Peter stood up, looked at Jesus and said to Him,

"Lord, if it is you, call me out onto the water with you."

Jesus replied, "Peter, come out on to the water."

With that, Peter slowly climbed over the edge of the boat. The other disciples could hardly believe what they were seeing.

"What is Peter doing?" they thought, "he does realise that he's climbing out of a boat into deep water, right?"

Peter lowered himself over the boat onto the water, where his feet came to rest on the water's surface. Peter then walked on the water towards where Jesus was stood. And then, swoosh... the wind picked up and Peter became afraid and began to sink.

[Scene 5: Peter sinking in the water as he walks out to meet Jesus]

Reaching out his hand, Jesus grabbed Peter, stopping him from sinking.

"You of little faith. What happened? Why did you doubt?" said Jesus to Peter.

After the two of them climbed into the boat with the other gobsmacked disciples, the wind died down. All of the disciples, including Peter, could do nothing but bow down and worship Jesus saying,

"It must be true. You must be God's Son."

And so they continued on their journey until they reached the shore.

[Scene 6: The disciples (looking fairly awestruck) and Jesus in the boat sailing to dry land]

TRUSTING GOD

NAME ....

♪ I'm gonna fully rely on God... Trust him with all I've got! ♪

Psst... Can you remember what **F R O G** stands for?

F ....
R ....
O ....
G ....

Can we rely on God for everything?

Does that mean we don't need to revise for tests?

Write loads of amazing things about God here to remind you that he's worth relying on!

GOD

What was Peter thinking...

... when he was out 'walking' on the sea?!

How can we show God that we trust him with everything?

Write/draw your ideas here!

Thank God that we can **ALWAYS** rely on him.

PRAY! AMEN!

BIG STORY

Peter and the disciples were in a boat on the lake. Jesus went to meet them, walking ON the water. Peter stepped out and walked on water too! And when he got scared and started to sink, **Jesus saved him. Phew!**

Matthew 14: 22–34

He said WHAT?!

Jesus said, "You of little faith."

But Peter had just stepped out onto the water... isn't that BIG faith?!

CHECK IT OUT!

Proverbs 3: 5

So... what's the point in learning anything?

PUZZLE CORNER

IT'S AGAINST THE CLOCK!
You've got 2 MINUTES!

It's WORDSEARCH time!

R	H	E	U	A	T	W
E	T	S	N	T	A	U
T	I	E	U	L	O	O
E	A	O	K	S	B	T
P	F	I	O	T	E	C
W	N	R	E	L	Y	J
G	T	R	U	S	T	L

Peter
Boat
Jesus
Trust
Walking
Faith
Rely

WHO IS JESUS?

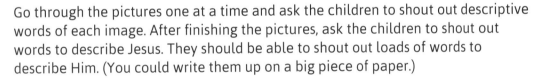

WORDS ARE NOT ENOUGH

 PLAY IT

7-10 mins

You will need:

- Paper
- Pens/ pencils
- A list of things to draw (anything at all)

Play a game of 'Draw-it!':

Split the children into teams and give each team a few sheets of paper and a pen. Ask one child from each team to come up to you and then tell them what the first 'thing' on the list is. They must then go back to their teams and draw the 'thing' without talking. The rest of the team must guess what it is and, once guessed correctly, the next person from each team goes up, tells you what the previous picture was, and receives the next 'thing' to draw. It's a race to the end; the first team to guess all of the pictures correctly wins!

 INTRO IT

4 mins

You will need:

- 10 different pictures of things that are not too difficult to describe. For example, a wooden table, lightning, a tropical fish, a house
- *(Optional)* Large piece of paper and pens

Go through the pictures one at a time and ask the children to shout out descriptive words of each image. After finishing the pictures, ask the children to shout out words to describe Jesus. They should be able to shout out loads of words to describe Him. (You could write them up on a big piece of paper.)

Explain to the children that it is impossible to fully describe God, because of who He is. We do know things about God though, and a lot of these we see from looking at Jesus. So, today we're looking at *Who is Jesus?*

 SING IT

5 mins

You will need:

- *God's Love Is Unstoppable* album and facilities to play it

Sing *Words Are Not Enough* together (Track 6).

Song actions can be found at *www.bigministries.co.uk.*

 TELL IT

7 mins

You will need:

- Story script (starting on page 29)

Teach the children the trigger words and encourage them to interact as you tell them the story.

You will need:

- An activity sheet copied for each child (on page 32)
- Pens/pencils
- Bibles

10-13 mins

Go through the sheet - use it as a foundation for discussion. Allow the children to do the sheet however they would like to, but talk to them about the key questions as they are doing things.

 You will need:

- Everything to make a stained glass window!
- Choose whether you want to buy a ready-to-go pack or create your own. Look on Baker Ross (search for 'stained glass') for ideas

10 mins

 **You will need:**

- Your piece of paper with words on from 'Intro it' (if you did this!)

5-10 mins

Play a game similar to the classic 'concentration.'

Sit in a circle.

As a reference, stick up the sheet of words describing Jesus.

The rhythm is created by slapping both hands on your thighs, then a clap, then clicking each hand. As you do each 'noise' you say a word or two:

Who [*slap thighs*] is [*clap*] Je- [*one click*] -sus [*one click*]

Can you [*slap thighs*] tell me [*clap*] who He [*one click*] is [*one click*]?

A child then responds with something along the lines of:

Jesus [*slap thighs*] is [*clap*] awe- [*one click*] -some [*one click*]

You then repeat the call, and ask a different child to respond.

If your group are particularly good at this, you could try to get them to go one after another with no 'rhythm' gap or 'call' from you in-between!

Keep the rhythm going at all times!

THE TRANSFIGURATION

(Matthew 17:1-13; Mark 9:2-13; Luke 9:28-36)

INSTRUCTIONS At various points throughout this story try to encourage the children to think about how the disciples were feeling. Get them to pull the different facial expressions of the disciples as they went on this journey and teach them this trigger phrase:

Are we nearly there yet: 'NOT YET!'

"This way," Jesus beckoned to the others, "follow me".

"Where are we going?" asked Peter trying to catch his breath. "**Are we nearly there yet**?"

Peter was being followed closely behind by James and John who were clambering their way over rocks and loose stones.

Jesus raised His arm and pointed upwards; upwards to the top of a high mountain.

"That's where we're going!" He said.

Peter, James and John hung their heads, all of them thinking the exact same thing—"That's a long way up." But, onward and upward they went. It didn't matter how far it was; they were willing to follow Jesus anywhere.

Over rocks and under rocks, through gentle streams and squelching mud... up and up and up the mountain they travelled.

"**Are we nearly there yet?**" called one of the disciples.

They weren't. And so they continued, over rocks and under rocks, through gentle streams and squelching mud... up and up and up the mountain they travelled.

And then came the same question,

"**Are we nearly there yet?**"

And were they? Nope. Not quite yet... And so they continued, over rocks and under rocks, through gentle streams and squelching mud... up and up and up the mountain they travelled.

"Are we nearly th... "

"We're there!" said Jesus interrupting.

Jesus, Peter, James and John stood at the top of the very high mountain. There was no-one else around, no-one to be seen. They were alone. While the disciples stood there, feeling worn out, breathless and confused as to the purpose of this strenuous up-hill hike, Jesus' clothes began to brighten—and not the sort of brightness you get from the sun on a bright sunny day.
Jesus' clothes became a dazzling blinding white, shining from the top of the mountain.

"What's happening?" the disciples asked one another.

And then, two people appeared next to Jesus. It was Moses and Elijah, speaking with Jesus, whose clothes remained a dazzling bright white.

What does one do in this situation? What would you think was going on? Peter's instant reaction was to say this...

"Lord, it's good that we're here. Shall I build three shelters? One for you, Moses and Elijah?"

Peter didn't know what else to say or do. There just weren't any words or actions to match up to what was happening on top of this mountain. Not to mention that Peter, James and John were frozen with fear at this strange occurrence.

As if they weren't scared enough already, a cloud then covered the disciples and a voice came from within the cloud.

"This is my Son, whom I love. Listen to Him!"

Still frozen with fear, the disciples were now curled up on the floor with their eyes closed, faces to the ground with their hands over their heads.

Jesus approached the three of them and, touching them on their heads, they opened their eyes and looked up.

"Don't be afraid" said Jesus calmly.

As Peter, James and John looked around they could see no one else. Moses and Elijah were no longer there and the cloud that covered them had disappeared. There was only Jesus left.

Jesus, Peter, James and John then made their way down the mountainside, over rocks and under rocks, through gentle streams and squelching mud... down and down and down the mountain they travelled.

"**Are we nearly there yet?**" came a voice from the back.

On the way down, Jesus told the three of them to keep what they had seen a secret.
They weren't to tell anyone until after He had died and risen again.
And so, Peter, James and John kept everything they'd seen
to themselves until the time that Jesus had said.

WHO IS JESUS?

NAME

BIG STORY

Psst... This story is called The Transfiguration!

Jesus took Peter, James & John up a mountain. When they got to the top, Jesus' clothes started to glow and Moses & Elijah appeared.

God spoke: **"This is my Son, listen to him."** Then everything returned to normal. Weird!

Luke 9: 28-36

Have you ever built a **shelter** or **den outside?**

Have you ever **slept out** in a shelter?

Why did he want to build shelters?

What was Peter thinking?

PUZZLE CORNER

How many words can you make from these letters?

2 MINUTES

JESUS' TRANSFIGURATION

Jesus said, **"Don't be afraid!"**

REALLY? Would you have been scared?

What is joy?

Peter was **so excited** about what was happening, **he didn't know what to do!** Sometimes when we are worshipping God, we just can't think of what to say because he's **so awesome...** That's when we can use our **actions** to tell God **how great he is.**

What's your favourite thing to do to worship God? Write/draw it here!

♫ Words are not enough to tell you, God, how we really feel about you! ♫

CHECK IT OUT!

John 1

Psst... Jesus is "The Word"!

This BIG STORY is a bit *weird...* **What do you think was going on?** Why were Moses & Elijah there?

Write some things about **Jesus** here.

Jesus is...

DRAW THE DISCIPLES' FACES WHEN THEY SAW JESUS, MOSES & ELIJAH!

*How do we **know** these things?*

PRAY!

Thank Jesus for being awesome!

AMEN!

SERVING OTHERS

 You will need:

- A 'pass the parcel' ready to go

5-8 mins

Time to have some fun! Play *Pass the Parcel* with your group.

 You will need:

- Drinks
- Cakes
- Biscuits   **5 mins**
- Aprons
- Note books
- Napkins

Set up a 'café'. Have a selection of drinks and cakes / biscuits available. You could even have a till set up if you have that sort of thing available to you.

Choose some of the children to be waiters or waitresses. Try and make them look the part by giving them aprons and notebooks, then get them to serve the other children. (If you have a small group, the children could serve your leaders.)

Tell the children that today we are thinking about *Serving Others*.

Sometimes it's fun (like in a pretend café like this) to serve others, other times it's harder to do, but Jesus asks us to serve others like He did.

 You will need:

- Story script (starting on page 36)
- A bowl of water   **7 mins**
- A towel
- Drinks and snacks

Read through the story beforehand so that you are familiar with it. Get the children to follow along with the interaction as you instruct.

 You will need:

- *God's Love Is Unstoppable* album and facilities to play it   **5 mins**

Sing *So Much Fun* together (Track 7).

Song actions can be found at *www.bigministries.co.uk*.

You will need:

10-13 mins

- An activity sheet copied for each child (on page 38)
- Pens/pencils
- Bibles

Go through the sheet - use it as a foundation for discussion. Allow the children to do the sheet however they would like to, but talk to them about the key questions as they are doing things.

This will flow straight into the 'Respond to it' time.
If you choose Option 1 in 'Create it', use Option 1 in 'Respond to it'.
If you choose Option 2 in 'Create it', use Option 2 in 'Respond to it'.

5-7 mins

[OPTION 1] (Only for the brave!)
You will need:

- Paints
- Paper

Create some angel paintings, using foot and hand prints of the children!

Use a foot print (toes to the bottom of the piece of paper) to make a body of an angel, and then do a hand print either side for the wings. Then paint on a simple head (just a circle above the 'heel' of the footprint) with a halo above it.

It would look really good with white paint on black sugar paper.

[OPTION 2]
You will need:

8-12 mins

- Flip flops (one per child)
- Goggly eyes
- Strips of wool
- Pipe cleaners
- Stick-on shapes
- Anything else decorative

Make a flip flop monster puppet! Use the thongs of the flip flop to tie hair (wool) onto, and add eyes (goggly eyes) below this—the more the better, they'll look crazy! Then invite the children to decorate their flip flop monster however they like!

[OPTION 1]
You will need:

4 mins

- A bowl of water
- Towels

If you did [OPTION 1] in 'Create it', then use this as an opportunity for the children to 'serve' each other by helping to wash each others hands and feet!

Talk about the fact that we wouldn't normally have a need to wash each others' hands and feet! However, today it is one way we can serve each other as we are all messy! In the time that Jesus walked on the earth, He and His disciples would have walked in sandals and would have had REALLY grubby feet.

[OPTION 2]
If you did [OPTION 2] in *'Create it'*, then this is the response for you!

This sort of craft often makes a lot of mess. Ask the children to practise serving by helping clear up (making sure they sort the recycling from the rubbish!).

The simple responses are often the best. Reward them for their help with some sort of treat!

JESUS WASHES THE DISCIPLES' FEET
(John 13:1-17)

Peter and the other disciples had now been with Jesus for some time, following Him wherever He went and listening to His every word. Jesus' time on this earth was almost at an end. He came from God and was soon to be on His way back to God.

Jesus and the disciples were all sat around a table preparing for the Passover feast.

> *[Get the children sitting around a table together and hand out some food to them. It's up to you which food. You can go for a full Passover feast or just some biscuits and drinks. They can eat or drink as you read the rest of the story.]*

As everyone sat there, Jesus stood up, took off His outer robe, and put it to one side. In place of it, He wrapped a towel around His waist and began filling up a bowl with water.

Carrying the bowl over to where the disciples were sat eating and chatting, Jesus got on to His knees and began washing the disciples' feet. One at a time He went around the table, washing feet and drying them with the towel.

> *[At this point in the story you could go around and wash each child's feet (hands if you'd prefer. Hands might be a simpler, easier option).]*

Jesus then pushed the bowl of water over to where Peter was sat and knelt down at his feet.

"Jesus, are you going to wash my feet?" Peter asked.

"Peter, you don't realise what I'm doing," replied Jesus, "but later, you'll get it."

"You shall NEVER wash my feet, Jesus," Peter answered, adamant that Jesus would not go near his feet.

But then Jesus spoke these words to Peter, "Peter, unless I wash you, you have no part with me."

Peter then, suddenly, changed his tune.

"Well then don't just wash my feet, but my hands, my head as well... all of me!"

"Peter," said Jesus once again, "anyone that has had a bath need only to wash their feet. Their whole body is already clean."

Jesus then finished washing Peter's feet, put on His clothes and returned to His place at the table.

Everyone then stopped eating, their eyes fixed on Jesus, and they listened as He spoke these words,

"Do you all understand what I've done for you? You all call me teacher and master, which is correct. So, if I, the teacher and master, wash your feet, you all must now do to each other as I have done for you, and wash each others' feet."

> *[At this point in the story give the children the option of taking it in turns to wash each others' feet or hands.]*

"No servant is greater than his master," Jesus continued, "nor is a messenger greater than the one who sent him with a message. If you understand what I've told you, then act on it and you will be blessed."

And they continued with the Passover meal, for very soon Jesus was to be betrayed and handed over to be crucified.

SERVING OTHERS

NAME

HUMILITY
Do you know what that means?

Every action is a way of showing... I love God and I love that he loves me!

CHURCH IS FUN

Your ideas

Washing people's feet

Your ideas

He said WHAT ?!

Jesus said, "Anyone who's had a bath only needs to wash their feet!"

What?

AMEN!

What do you think?
What things does Jesus think are most important?

Praying for the poor and sick

Giving money to charity

Your ideas

loving people

I'M RICH

SO... If we follow Jesus, do we need to wash people's feet?

Ask God to help us **serve others** just like Jesus did.

PRAY!

Have you ever walked on a **really dusty road** wearing **sandals**?

CHECK IT OUT!

Mark 10: 44

What can we do to **serve others**? Write/draw your ideas here!

What was Peter thinking? Why didn't he want Jesus to wash his feet? (I don't think it's just 'cos he didn't like his feet being touched!)

BIG STORY
Peter and the disciples were all together for the Passover* feast. Jesus started to **wash all the disciples' feet.** Peter wouldn't let him wash his. Jesus said, "unless I wash your feet, you have no part with me!" Peter then wanted Jesus to wash his **whole body!!**

John 13

*Psst... The **Passover** was a meal when Jewish people remembered how God looked after them in Egypt, and protected them from terrible plagues.*

PUZZLE CORNER

IT'S AGAINST THE CLOCK!
You've got 1 MINUTE!

Which tap will fill the jar?

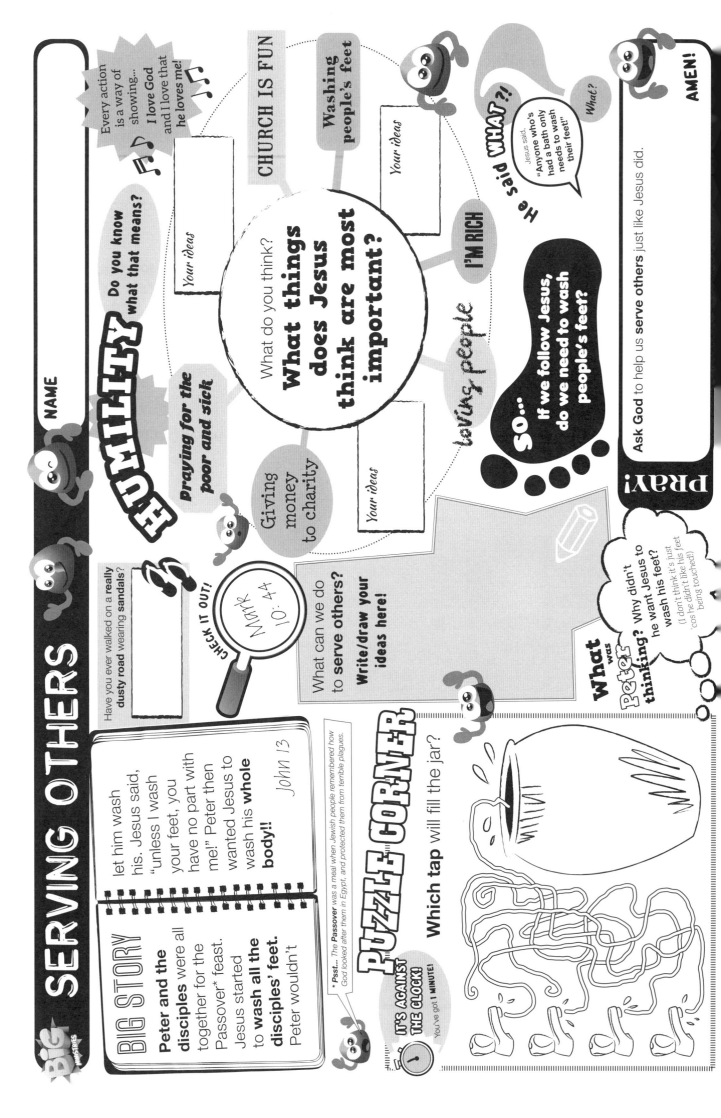

FORGIVENESS

I TURN TO YOU

 PLAY IT

7 mins

You will need:

- A piece of paper for each child
- A pen / pencil for each child

Split into two teams.

Get each of the children to write three things on their piece of paper: two things about themselves that are false, and one thing about themselves that is true.

When everybody has done this, ask the first child on one team to read aloud the three options that they've written, without giving away which one's true and which are false. The other team must then guess which is true.

If they guess correctly they get a point. It is then the next team's turn for one child to read aloud their three options and for the other team to guess.

 INTRO IT

5 mins

You will need:

- A chalk board
- Some chalk
- A sponge / board rubber (make sure it's dry!)

Tell the children that today we are thinking about *Forgiveness*.

Use a chalk board and invite the children to write on it things they don't like (anything at all, like sprouts or homework!).

Use the board rubber and rub them out.

Talk about the fact that when you rub out chalk writing like this, the chalk board is still marked with the chalk dust.

When we forgive people there is often something left... we don't easily forget about what happened, even if we've decided to forgive people.

Tell the children that it's not like that for God. When He forgives, He completely forgets! When we ask Him to forgive us He really will!

Read this from Ephesians 4:32: 'Be kind and compassionate to one another, forgiving each other, just as in Christ God forgave you.'

There's a challenge!

TELL IT

7 mins

You will need:

• Story script (starting on page 42)

There's no specified interaction for this story so you'll need to make sure you know it well and can make it come to life. Read over the story a few times so that you are familiar with it.

You could ask the children to find a space to lie down, close their eyes and imagine all the scenes as they listen to you read the story.

 SING IT

5 mins

You will need:

• *God's Love Is Unstoppable* album and facilities to play it

Sing *I Turn To You* together (Track 8).

Song actions can be found at *www.bigministries.co.uk*.

 TALK ABOUT IT

10-13 mins

You will need:

• An activity sheet copied for each child (on page 44)
• Pens/pencils
• Bibles

Go through the sheet - use it as a foundation for discussion. Allow the children to do the sheet however they would like to, but talk to them about the key questions as they are doing things.

 CREATE IT

7-12 mins

You will need:

• Cardboard tubes (a third of a kitchen roll inner per child)
• Pens
• Pipe-cleaners (preferably orange, white and red!)
• Glue
• Sticky Tape
• *Optional:* White paint

We are going to make a cardboard tube cockerel!

These will work without painting the tube, but if you have time, paint the tube inside and out with white paint.

Cut an orange pipe cleaner in half and use to make two legs. Tape one end on the inside of the tube, and make the other end into a foot shape.

Cut a white pipe cleaner in half, create a heart shape, and tape them onto the sides of the tube for the wings.

Cut a red pipe cleaner in half, and create a shape with three points for the cockerel's comb. Tape this onto the inside top of the tube.

Decorate the face with eyes and a beak, and you have a cockerel!

For more details search for *Chicken Tube* at this website:

http://craftsbyamanda.com

You will need:

5 mins

- Small pieces of paper
- Pens
- Bin / bin bag

Give each child a piece of paper and a pen.

Invite them to write on their piece of paper anything that they would like to ask God to forgive them for.

Then get the children to either screw up their paper, or tear it up and throw it away in the bin. As the children do this, read to them Psalm 103:12.

Remind them that when we ask God for forgiveness, He forgives and forgets.

Tell the children you will dispose of the bin bag properly as a symbol that it is completely gone!

PETER'S DENIAL
(John 18:1-27)

"Peter, before the cockerel crows, you will disown me three times," said Jesus to Peter as they sat around the Passover table.

"Never, Jesus," Peter replied, "I would never disown you."

After Jesus had finished speaking and praying with His disciples, they left where they were and walked a short way to a garden called Gethsemane. It was a garden that they often visited.

It was here that Judas Iscariot, one of Jesus' disciples, led the Roman soldiers to arrest Jesus. It was here that Judas Iscariot betrayed Jesus for 30 pieces of silver.

As the soldiers approached Jesus, Peter, filled with passion and wanting to defend Him, drew his sword, raised it high in the air and launched it at the servant of the High Priest who was also there to arrest Jesus. The sword narrowly missed the High Priest's head catching his ear on the way down, slicing it clean off!

"Stop Peter! Put your sword away," Jesus commanded, "no more of this!"

And He touched the ear of the man, instantly healing him.

The Roman soldiers and guards then arrested Jesus, binding His wrists together, and they took Him away. As the soldiers led Jesus away, Peter and another disciple followed close behind, eager to know what was to happen to their friend and teacher.

Jesus was taken in to see the High Priest, whose name was Caiaphas, but Peter was allowed to go no further.

"What are they going to do with Him?" Peter said to himself, "What are they going to do with Jesus?"

Peter hung around outside the courtyard of the High Priest, pacing up and down, fidgeting nervously, his thoughts racing.

Eventually, a servant girl who was on duty in the courtyard brought Peter in.

"Are you...? You are aren't you!? You're one of Jesus' followers."

"No!" replied Peter as quick as anything, "No, I'm not. What are you talking about?"

Peter quickly shuffled away to a nearby fire to keep himself warm. Standing around the fire were some of the High Priest's servants and guards.

"Excuse me," said one of the men standing around the fire, "aren't you one of Jesus' disciples?"

"No!" said Peter quite sternly.

And then a relative of the man who's ear Peter had recently cut off said,

"I'm sure you are…. Didn't I see you in the garden when He was arrested?"

"No, no, NO!" shouted Peter, "I'm not His follower. Leave me alone."

Just then, a cockerel crowed. Peter's face dropped as he remembered what Jesus had said to him;

"Before the cockerel crows today you will disown me three times."

Peter then ran out of the courtyard and, ashamed of himself and all alone, he cried bitterly.

BIG STORY

Jesus was **arrested.** Peter managed to cut off one of the soldiers' ears... which Jesus then **healed!**

Jesus was taken away, and Peter pretended three times that he **didn't know Jesus** when people asked him.

John 18: 1–27

PUZZLE CORNER

IT'S AGAINST THE CLOCK! You've got 1 MINUTE!

Dot-to-dot time!

I want to start again, Jesus, and walk right by your side. ♪

How many times can we turn away from God before he gives up on us?

Have you ever been given an **amazing present? Draw it here!**

So... What is sin?

Do you find it easy to tell your friends that you follow Jesus? What would help?

He said **WHAT?!**

Jesus said, **"You will disown me 3 times."**

What does "disown" mean?

Why did he pretend he didn't know Jesus?

What was Peter thinking?

FORGIVEN!

1 John 1: 9

CHECK IT OUT!

AMEN!

Colour in the word!

PRAY!

Is there anything you want God to **forgive** you for? **Why not ask him,** now?

GOD'S LOVE IS UNSTOPPABLE

UNSTOPPABLE

 PLAY IT

5-10 mins

You will need:

- Two small paddling pools filled with water, or ball-pool balls
- Tiny toy fish or laminated card fish
- Some sort of 'pincers' or fishing rods to retrieve the fish! (You could perhaps attach magnets to the fish, and make a mini magnetic fishing rod!)

This is a relay race to see which team can collect the most fish.

Get each team to stand in a line. The first person must run to the pool, collect a fish and bring it back to their line and join the back of the queue. The next person then goes and does the same. Set a time limit and see which team has won at the end of the time.

You could even add obstacles to make it more of a challenge to get to the pool.

 INTRO IT

5 mins

You will need:

- A can of 'squirty cream'
- A biscuit
- A plate

Tell the children that the theme that we're thinking about today is *God's love*.

Read this verse from 1 John 3:1: 'See what great love the Father has lavished on us that we should be called children of God. And that is what we are!'

Ask the children if they know what the word 'lavished' means, get them to chat about it!

Tell the children that God lavishing His love on us is a bit like this:

Place a biscuit on a plate. Take the 'squirty cream' and add a little bit to the biscuit. Then a little bit more.... and then empty the entire contents of the can onto the biscuit!

So it's not a complete waste of cream, give everyone a biscuit (or even a British strawberry if they're in season) and get them to dip it into the cream. As they're eating, tell the children that God will keep giving us His love no matter what and, unlike the can of cream, His love will never run out.

 TELL IT

7 mins

You will need:

- Story script (starting on page 47)

Teach the children the trigger words and encourage them to interact as you tell them the story.

You will need:

5 mins

- *God's Love Is Unstoppable* album and facilities to play it

Sing *Unstoppable* together (Track 4).

Song actions can be found at *www.bigministries.co.uk*.

 You will need:

10-13 mins

- An activity sheet copied for each child (on page 50)
- Pens/pencils
- Bibles

Go through the sheet - use it as a foundation for discussion. Allow the children to do the sheet however they would like to, but talk to them about the key questions as they are doing things.

 You will need:

7-12 mins

- Plastic bottle (with no lid) for each child
- Different coloured string / wool - cut in long lengths
- PVA glue
- Card
- Pens

We are going to make a mini bottle vase with an unending thread around!

Cover the plastic bottle in a thin layer of PVA glue.

Starting at the bottom of the bottle get the children to carefully wrap the string around the bottle, making sure one 'round' sits directly on top of the 'round' below. Continue to wrap the entire bottle like this, then tuck the thread into the top and make sure it's glued in. You should now not be able to see any of the bottle.

If you have time for it to dry, cover the string in an additional layer of PVA. This will give it a bit of a shine but will take a while to dry.

Now get the children to design a label with a reminder on it that God's love is never ending. Finally, stick the label on the bottle.

 **You will need:**

6-8 mins

- Plain biscuits
- Water icing
- Writing icing
- Sweets and sprinkles!

Get the children to decorate the biscuits. Topping them finally with an eternity symbol or the words 'God's love never ends'.

Tell the children that they are to give their biscuits away to someone they love! (Just like Jesus made and shared food in the story we heard today.)

THE AMAZING CATCH OF FISH / JESUS REINSTATES PETER
(John 21)

"We've been out all night, we must have caught something?" said one of the disciples tired from the long night.

"Nope," Peter responded, "**Nothing**. We've been out here all night and caught **nothing**."

Now, it was early in the morning when a man appeared, standing on the shore. The sun was rising and the disciples had just about given up.

Putting his hands up to his mouth, the man shouted with all he could muster,

"Friends! Have you caught any **fish**!?"

The disciples, annoyed, all joined together in shouting back,

"NO! **NOTHING**!"

"Take your nets," the man shouted, "and throw them over the right side of the boat!"

"He wants us to throw them over the right side of the boat?" asked one of the disciples, "Is he kidding? It's not going to make the slightest bit of difference. We've been here all night and caught **nothing**."

After a short discussion as to what the point of this would be, the disciples decided that they would play along with the man's request. As if they would catch any **fish** by just throwing their nets over the other side of the boat. They had been out at sea for a long long time and had caught **nothing**! But this wasn't just anybody. What the disciples hadn't realised was that this man, stood on the shore of Lake Galilee, was Jesus.

Jesus had died, risen to life and had already appeared to the disciples showing them the nail marks in His hands and feet. But at this moment on Lake Galilee, they didn't recognise that it was Him.

The disciples gathered the nets, took them to the right side of the boat, and hurled them over the edge... expecting to, once again, catch **nothing**.

Immediately the nets filled with large **fish**—153 **fish** to be exact.

As this happened, Peter realised that it was Jesus on the shore.

"It's Jesus. It's Jesus! Look!"

Taking off his fishing overalls, Peter jumped out of the boat into the cold salty water and made his way to Jesus on the shore. The other disciples followed close behind in the boat, along with the immense catch of **fish**.

All of the disciples finally reached the shore and, after dragging the huge net of **fish**, which surprisingly wasn't ripped or torn, onto the beach, they found Jesus sitting next to a fire that He had made, with bread and **fish** cooking on it.

"Bring the **fish** that you've caught and have breakfast with me," said Jesus.

They sat together and Jesus handed out the bread and **fish**. After they'd finished eating, Jesus turned to Peter.

"Peter, do you love me?" he asked.

"Yes Lord, you know I love you," Peter answered.

Jesus said to Peter, "Feed my lambs."

Again Jesus asked, "Peter, do you love me?"

Surprised that Jesus was asking him again, Peter again answered,

"Yes Lord, you know I love you."

Jesus said to Peter, "Take care of my sheep."

A third time, Jesus turned to Peter saying,

"Peter, do you love me?"

Peter was upset at this. He had already answered Jesus twice.

"Lord, you know all things," Peter said, "You know that I love you."

Jesus said to Peter, "Feed my sheep. Follow me."

After he had denied that he knew Jesus three times before Jesus died, Peter was forgiven and followed Jesus from then on, never again denying that he knew Him.

And so they continued eating bread and **fish**, all amazed at knowing Jesus; all amazed at how much their lives had changed since that first time they met Him.

Where did everyone go?

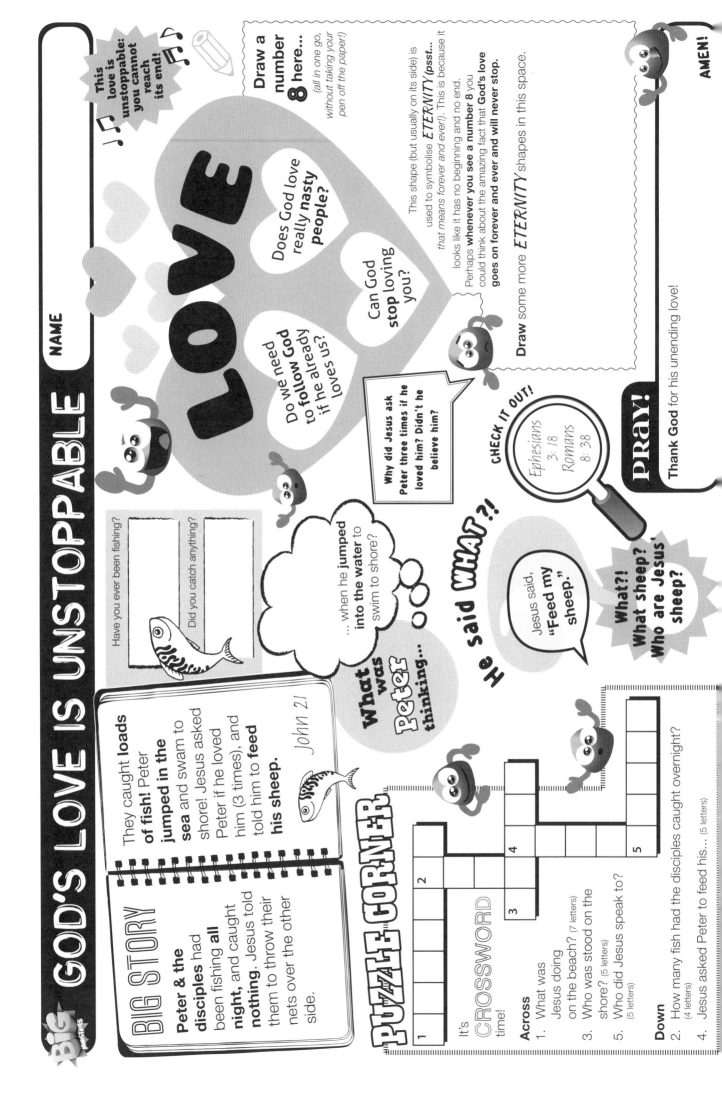

GOD'S LOVE IS UNSTOPPABLE

NAME

This love is unstoppable: you cannot reach its end!

BIG STORY

Peter & the disciples had been fishing **all night**, and caught **nothing**. Jesus told them to throw their nets over the other side.

They caught **loads of fish!** Peter **jumped in the sea** and swam to shore! Jesus asked Peter if he loved him (3 times), and told him to **feed his sheep.**

John 21

Have you ever been fishing?

Did you catch anything?

What was Peter thinking...

... when he jumped **into the water** to swim to shore?

He said WHAT?!

Jesus said, **"Feed my sheep."**

What?! What sheep? Who are Jesus' sheep?

Why did Jesus ask Peter three times if he loved him? Didn't he believe him?

Does God love really nasty **people?**

Can God **stop** loving **you?**

Do we need to **follow God** if he already loves us?

This shape (but usually on its side) is used to symbolise *ETERNITY (psst... that means forever and ever!)*. This is because it looks like it has no beginning and no end. Perhaps **whenever you see a number 8** you could think about the amazing fact that **God's love goes on forever and ever and will never stop.**

Draw some more *ETERNITY* shapes in this space.

Draw a number 8 here...

(all in one go, without taking your pen off the paper!)

CHECK IT OUT!
Ephesians 3:18
Romans 8:38

PRAY!
Thank God for his unending love!

AMEN!

PUZZLE CORNER

It's CROSSWORD time!

Across
1. What was Jesus doing on the beach? (7 letters)
3. Who was stood on the shore? (5 letters)
5. Who did Jesus speak to? (5 letters)

Down
2. How many fish had the disciples caught overnight? (4 letters)
4. Jesus asked Peter to feed his... (5 letters)

THE HOLY SPIRIT'S POWER

HELP US TO SHINE

 PLAY IT

5-8 mins

What you need:

- A suitably clear space
- A whistle

Play some mini-wrestling games! There are some ideas below but play whatever games you're comfortable leading (bear in mind the age and gender of your particular group).

Lay down the rules at the beginning. If people hear a whistle they should stop what they're doing immediately.

A few ideas for mini-wrestling games:

1. Arm wrestling

2. Thumb wars

3. Stand up!

> Two opponents sit on the floor with their knees bent and their toes touching those of the opponent.
>
> You will need a pole of some kind (like a broom handle). The pole is held by both opponents, with their hands alternating. There should be a short space in the middle between the hands.
>
> The object of the game is to pull the opponent up and over the dividing pole line - ultimately, make your opponent stand up!

4. Team tug of war

> NB: Each child will need to be wearing a long-sleeved top and gloves to participate in this game.

 INTRO IT

5 mins

You will need:

- A large fan (or a lot of small hand held fans)
- Lots of small pieces of paper / confetti

Use the fans to blow the small pieces of paper and get the children to have their hair blown by the wind of a fan.

Just for fun, you could throw various items of differing weights into the path of a big fan (paper / sponge / crisps) to see what the fan will blow away. Squirting a water pistol into the air flow might be fun too!

Tell the children that, although we couldn't see the wind that the fan created, we could see its effects on the things that came into contact with it.

Tell the children that today we're thinking about the *Holy Spirit's power*. The power of the Holy Spirit is a bit like the wind we've just been playing with! We can't see His power, but we can definitely see the effects.

You will need:

9 mins

- Story script (starting on page 54)
- Three big cards (large pieces of cardboard with A, B and C written on them)

Stick the three letters up around the room (alternatively, give them to three leaders if you have them, and they can move around!)

Throughout the story there are options to give the children, with three answers to choose from - A, B and C. Get the children to run to the letter that they think gives the correct answer.

 You will need:

5 mins

- *God's Love Is Unstoppable* album and facilities to play it

Sing *Help Us To Shine* together (Track 9).

Song actions can be found at *www.bigministries.co.uk*.

 You will need:

10-13 mins

- An activity sheet copied for each child (on page 56).
- Pens/pencils
- Bibles

Go through the sheet - use it as a foundation for discussion. Allow the children to do the sheet however they would like to, but talk to them about the key questions as they are doing things.

 You will need:

10 mins

- Brown and white bread
- Star cutters - quite a few different sizes
- A selection of sandwich fillings
- Knives
- Paper plates
- Clingfilm
- Little 'flags' for sandwiches with 'shine like a star for Jesus' written on them

Make sandwiches with the children - always a fun activity in itself!

Get the children to make two full slice sandwiches with the same filling (or at least complementary fillings!) one in brown bread and one in white. Once the sandwiches are complete the children need to cut out star shapes using the cutters - two or three stars from each sandwich - do exactly the same with both sandwiches.

Next, swap over the star shapes so you have white stars in the brown sandwich and vice versa!

Pop them onto a paper plate, cover them with clingfilm and stick a small flag in them with the words 'Help us to shine' written on. They can eat them later!

You will need:

- Small glow-in-the-dark stars (stickers or plastic stars are widely available)

Ask the children to take a star and to keep it with them as a reminder that the Holy Spirit gives us power even though sometimes we do not always see it.

THE HOLY SPIRIT COMES AT PENTECOST
(Acts 2)

"Don't leave Jerusalem, but wait for the gift that my Father promised. When the Holy Spirit comes you will be my witnesses to the ends of the world."

These were Jesus' final words before... what?

- A)   Before Jesus broke bread and gave thanks for the wine?
- **B)   Before Jesus was taken up into the sky and hidden behind a cloud?**
- C)   Before Jesus opened all of His birthday presents?

The answer is B. Jesus said this before He was taken up into the sky. The disciples watched in wonder and awe as He was taken to be with God the Father.

Days passed and the disciples remained in Jerusalem just as Jesus had commanded. They were all gathered together in one place when, without any warning, there was a sound like a super strong raging wind.

"Where's that coming from?" they asked.

But no-one knew. The sound consumed the entire building. But what was it?

Was it...

- A)   The sound of a jet plane flying overhead?
- **B)   The sound of the Holy Spirit entering the building?**
- C)   The sound of a ferocious storm sent from heaven?

The answer is B. The Holy Spirit rapidly spread through the building like wildfire.

In Jerusalem at this time there were many Jews from across the world. They were speaking the many different languages of the many different countries they were from. When they heard the sound like that of a super strong raging wind, they came running to see what the commotion was. On arriving at the house where the disciples were, the people were amazed at what they heard. But what did they hear?

Did they hear...

- A)   Peter singing in a voice similar to that of Lady Ga Ga and rapping like Jay-Z.
- **B)   All of the disciples speaking in different languages that they'd never even spoken before.**
- C)   The sound of God's voice saying, 'This is my Son whom I love'.

The correct answer is B. Each person that was there could hear the disciples speaking in their own language. Everyone could understand what they were saying no matter where they were from.

"How are we able to understand these people?" said one person, "What's going on?" said another, "These guys are from Galilee but I know exactly what they're saying. They're speaking my language!"

The disciples spoke in many languages telling of God's amazing works and wonders. Some people couldn't quite work out was going on and assumed that they were drunk, but others were hooked on listening to their every word.

Peter then stood up and spoke to the humongous crowd of people that had gathered.

"Listen up everyone. What I'm about to say is for all of you..."

As Peter continued, the people listened. But what did Peter say?

Did he say...

A)   John baptised you with water, but I will baptise you with the Holy Spirit.
B)   The other day I went to the paper shop... but it had blown away.
C)   **He told them all about Jesus and how their lives could be changed.**

The correct answer is C. Peter spoke to them about Jesus, what Jesus had done, who He was, and how everyone can know Him and be saved. After he had finished speaking, about 3,000 people committed themselves to following Jesus and were baptised.

This was the beginning of the first church. But what were some of the things that the first church did?

A)   Did they play knock and run on all of the people's houses who weren't Christians and push banana skins through their letter boxes?
B)   Did they all sail to a small island to set up a church building for fear of any of the Jewish leaders finding them?
C)   **Did they eat together, pray together, worship God together and share their possessions with one another?**

The correct answer is C, and everyday more and more people were added to their number as word spread throughout the land.

HOLY SPIRIT'S POWER

NAME

Jesus, you are not a secret... If you were, I couldn't keep it! ♪♫

IS HE SCARY?!

Is the Holy Spirit God?

Like a battery gives power to a torch, so the Holy Spirit gives power to us! Only he never runs out!

Does he do the same things as he did in the story?

HOLY SPIRIT

What does he do?

What do you think about the Holy Spirit?

CHECK IT OUT!

Matthew 5: 14-15

How can we bring out the **"God colours"** in the world?

Is he the same as Jesus?

PRAY!

Ask God to send you his **Holy Spirit**, to help you **shine out** for him!

AMEN!

What's the **most exciting thing** anyone's ever told you?

Did you keep it a **secret?**

What's your **favourite thing** to do?

Can you do this to **shine for God?** How?

He said WHAT?!

Jesus said, **"You will be my witnesses."**

What does that mean?

BIG STORY

Jesus went up to heaven in front of his disciples and then **the Holy Spirit came and gave power** to them. The disciples did things they'd never done before – like speak in languages they'd never learnt! Peter then spoke to crowds of people and 3,000 committed to follow Jesus! **WOW!**   Acts 2

What was Peter thinking... ... when he stood up to talk to the masses?

PUZZLE CORNER

UNSCRAMBLE these words!

1   POSTTENCE

2   HET OLHY TRISPI

3   SOG'D WROEP

Big MINISTRIES

IS THERE A PROBLEM TOO BIG FOR GOD?

YOU NEED NOT FEAR

 INTRO IT

 5-7 mins

You will need:

- Some mini puzzles - such as wooden 'make a cube' puzzles and metal link puzzles (available from *The Entertainer* toyshop)

Get the children to have a go at solving the puzzles that you placed in front of them. Perhaps give them a time limit before they need to pass their puzzle on to the next person.

Tell the children that in Matthew 19:26 Jesus says that, "...with God all things are possible."

Today we are thinking about the question: *'Is there a problem too big for God?'*

Ask the children what they think.

 PLAY IT

 5-10 mins

You will need:

- A number of written clues, leading to other clues, and finally to the key to the 'treasure'! (For some great tips, search for 'writing a treasure hunt' on wikihow.com)
- A treasure box with a padlock and key
- Treasure - sweets, or whatever you feel appropriate

Create a treasure hunt (outside if it's at all possible) that leads to the key for the treasure padlock.

When they have completed the hunt, they've won the prize and can enjoy it!

 TELL IT

 10-15 mins

You will need:

- Story script (starting on page 60)
- Dressing up clothes (optional)
- Photocopies of the story scripts for each group

This story will involve you splitting your group into three groups.

Each group takes one part of the story of Peter's escape, rehearsing it and performing their own dramatic interpretation of it.

Challenge the children to think of the things the characters might say and the expressions on their faces.

You will need:

- *God's Love Is Unstoppable* album and facilities to play it

Sing *You Need Not Fear* together (Track 11).

Song actions can be found at *www.bigministries.co.uk*.

 You will need:

- An activity sheet copied for each child (on page 62)
- Pens/pencils
- Bibles

Go through the sheet - use it as a foundation for discussion. Allow the children to do the sheet however they would like to, but talk to them about the key questions as they are doing things.

 You will need:

- Two medium circular felt pom poms each
- Four pipe cleaners each
- Two goggly eyes each
- String
- PVA glue

Time to create a spider!

Put a blob of glue on the top of a pom pom. Lay your four pipe cleaners across the top of the pom pom, with the middle of each going through the glue - this will create the eight legs of your spider.

Next, squash the other pom pom on top of this (adding more glue if required) creating a 'leg sandwich' effect! You will need to get the children to hold this tight for a minute or so to allow the glue to dry enough to hold it all together.

Attach two goggly eyes to the top pom pom, as well as a length of string - the spider's dangling web!

Bend the legs to make your spider look more spidery!

Additional wool or string can be attached to the legs to add more scary hair if you want to. You could even add more eyes!

You will need:

- Strips of paper - a few for each child
- Pens / pencils
- A stapler

Give each child a few strips of paper and a pen. Ask them to write or draw on the strips of paper, things that they are scared of or worry about.

Get them to make a mini paper chain of their fears.

Then join everyone's chain up together to make one long chain, using a stapler.

Next, get all of the children to stand on one side of the room, and two leaders to hold up the chain, like a finishing line, across the middle of the room.

Say a prayer with the children, giving all these fears to God. As you say AMEN they should all run together at the chain and break it, symbolising that God is bigger than anything they fear!

PETER'S ESCAPE FROM PRISON
(Acts 12:1-17)

Peter's Escape From Prison: Part 1

Characters: Peter
The Angel of the Lord
Prison guards x 12 (or as many as you have to represent 12)

The church was continuing to grow in number every day but as their numbers grew, they began to find themselves in more and more danger.

King Herod discovered that the more Christians he arrested, the more popular he would become amongst the Jews. And so he did just that; he arrested Christians left, right and centre and even had some put to death, winning him even more favour among the people.

During this time of insanity, Peter also found himself arrested and thrown in a prison cell. The gates were firmly locked, the stone walls were thick and solid and the prison guards were tough and mean. In fact, there were 12 guards placed outside Peter's prison cell—12 tough and mean prison guards.

It was the night before Peter was to be brought out and put on trial. As Peter slept, snoring away, with the guards on watch, an angel visited him in the dark gloomy prison cell, and brightened the room up with a gleaming radiant glow.

Peter's Escape From Prison: Part 2

Characters: Peter
The Angel of the Lord
Prison guards x 12 (or as many as you have to represent 12)

In prison, with Peter chained up, the Angel of the Lord tapped Peter on his side in order to wake him up.

Peter's chains fell off his wrists and the angel told him to gather his clothes and put on his sandals.

The angel and Peter walked straight past all of the guards without being noticed. Some were sleeping and some were standing guard.

Peter and the Angel of the Lord came to a huge iron gate. Tall and wide and firmly fixed in position, shut tightly; no way in or out. But the gate just opened, all by itself.

Peter and the angel then walked straight through the gate, unnoticed. Peter was out of prison. He was free. The angel then left him to continue on his own. "I can hardly believe what just happened" Peter said to himself, pinching his arm to make sure that he wasn't dreaming, "God really is looking after me!"

Peter's Escape From Prison: Part 3

Characters: Peter
Young Girl
Mary and a group of Christians
The 'door'

Peter walked along the dusty roads to the house of a woman named Mary. He was still in an odd state of shock at being bust out of jail by an angel! Peter knocked on the door.

"Who is it?" came a young girl's voice from the other side. Peter said that it was him, but the girl ran off in such excitement she forgot to open the door.

Peter stood there waiting, shouting for someone to let him in.

Mary and the others had all been praying, and when they heard it was Peter at the door everyone rushed to greet him, hugging him and crying with joy.

"Sssshh, quiet down," said Peter, softly, "you will never guess what just happened to me." And as Peter told them of his miraculous escape from prison, they all praised God together.

IS THERE A PROBLEM TOO BIG FOR GOD?

NAME

Deuteronomy 31: 6

CHECK IT OUT!

He is bigger than anything you could dream of... He is a shield of love.

Draw a mini picture of the

BIGGEST THING

you've ever seen!

What do you do when things go *really* wrong? **Colour in** the things you do.

Clap

Cry

Read the Bible

Smile

Find Mum or Dad

Get cross

Go moody

Pray

Moan

Cheer

Hide

Throw stuff

Sing to God

Eat chocolate

Ignore everything

Have you ever been to see anyone **in prison?**

Have you ever seen an **angel?** Have any of your leaders?

When things are hard, it's easy for us to think that God isn't with us, or he doesn't care. Even sometimes when we don't feel like God's with us, we can KNOW he is, because **he promises to be.**

Reading the Bible helps with this because we can see all the **cool stories of God helping people** with all sorts of crazy problems! Praying helps too – we can talk to God, and **he will help!**

... as the angel woke him up?

What was Peter thinking...

WHAT'S THE SCARIEST THING THAT'S EVER HAPPENED TO YOU?

Thank God that we don't need to be afraid. **Ask him** to help us trust him.

PRAY!

Psst... Is there is no problem too big for God!

AMEN!

BIG STORY

Peter was in prison.
An **angel** came to rescue him and **led him out safely!**

He went to see the other disciples who were amazed and **praised God.**

Acts 12: 1–18

PUZZLE CORNER

1 MINUTE

Help Peter and the angel to **escape from prison!**

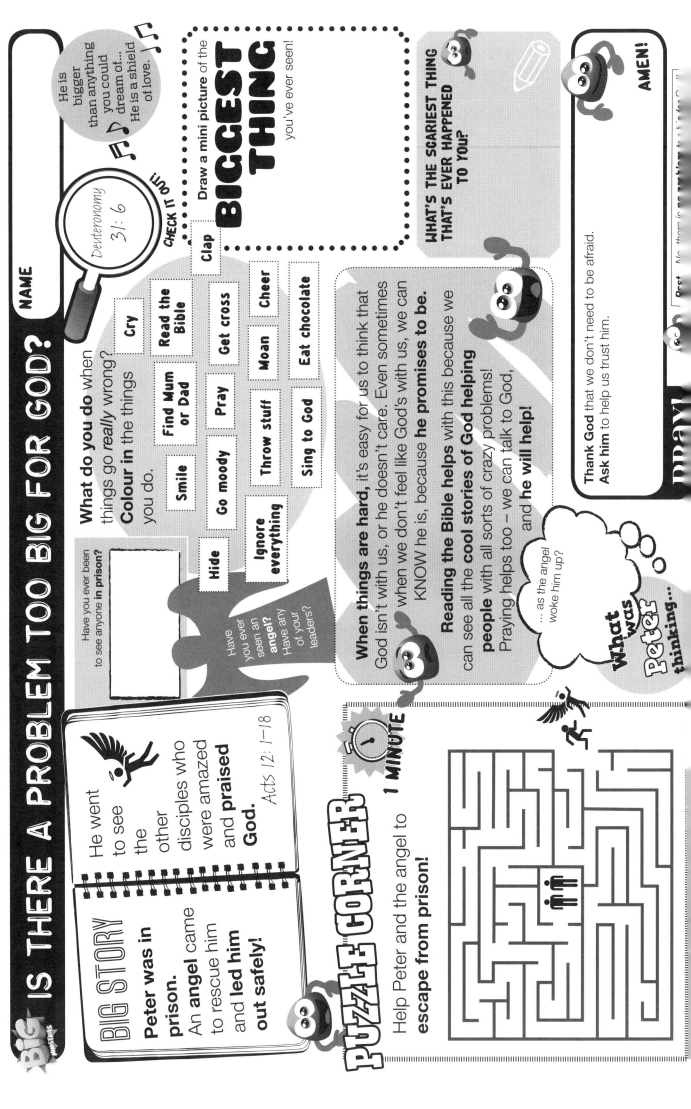

RHYTHM SESSION

 REATE IT [OPTION 1] **MAKE A DRUM**

15-20 mins

You will need:

- A 20-30cm tall section cut from a carpet tube per child
  (or some other kind of tough cylindrical tube)
- Fine sandpaper
- Balloons - one per child
- Scissors
- Glue
- Ribbon
- Fun, decorative sticky things (adhesive foam shapes are great)
- Coloured paper
- Strong sticky tape

How to make your drum:

1) Sand both ends of the tube with the sandpaper
   You will want to make it as smooth as possible so that the balloon doesn't pop
   when you put it on.

2) Cut the tail off the balloon.

3) Stretch the balloon over one end of the tube. (This may take two people!)

4) Stick the balloon on all the way around with strong sticky tape.

5) Decorate the drum.
   Ideas:
   - ribbons if you want a handle
   - stickers
   - tissue paper
   - paint if you'd like to make a mess!
   - paper if you want to cover the drum completely
   - arms and eyes if you want to make a drum man!

[OPTION 2] **MAKE A SHAKY EGG**

You will need:

- Plastic hollow eggs that open out in halves. Have a look on *www.bakerross.co.uk*
- Uncooked rice
- Sticky tape
- Tissue paper
- Glue - Not PVA
- Ribbon
- Fun, decorative sticky things
- Goggly eyes
- Pipe cleaners

How to make your shaky egg:

1) Fill the egg with as much rice as you want.
   Have a few tries with different amounts to get the sound you like best.

2) Tape the egg shut.

3) Cut up the tissue paper into squares / shapes and cover the whole egg.
   It's best to not use PVA glue as it takes too long to dry.

4) Decorate your shaky egg.
   Ideas:
   - stickers
   - eyes and pipe cleaner legs - make a bug!?
   - ribbon for 'tails' or to wrap around

 RHYTHM WORKSHOP [PART 1]

15 mins

You will need:

- Your drums or shaky eggs
- Everyone sitting in a circle

1) *Play That One Back*

   Play a rhythm with a drum and get them to all repeat it back to you at the same time with their instruments.

   After a few goes at this, move around the circle and ask each child, one at a time, to come up with their own rhythm that everyone else in the group must repeat.

   The only rule - keep the rhythms short!

2) *Don't Play That One Back*

   With everyone standing up in a circle, play a rhythm which is called the 'Don't Play That One Back' rhythm.

   This rhythm is the spoken rhythm of the phrase: Don't Play That One Back. It is a four-beat phrase. If you know muscial terms (or can find someone who does) this will help:

DON'T [crotchet] - PLAY [crotchet] - THAT ONE [quaver, quaver] BACK [crotchet]

Ultimately the game works by the leader playing a series of rhythms and the children repeating the rhythm. However, as the leader, you can every-so-often, play the 'Don't Play That One Back' rhythm. If anyone plays it back (or even just starts too) then they are out and must sit down.

3) *Crescendo and Diminuendo* [CHRISH-END-O and DIM-IN-YOU-END-O]

Ask the children if any of them know what a crescendo is...

Or a diminuendo?

The answers: Crescendo is a term used in music to mean gradually getting louder.

Diminuendo is a term used in music to mean gradually getting quieter.

With your rhythm instruments, practice your brand new skills in Crescendo and Diminuendo!

You could raise your arms to signal getting louder, and lower them to signal when everyone needs to play quieter.

 You will need:

5-10 mins

God's Love Is Unstoppable album and facilities to play it

Sing *Rhythm Inside* together (Track 5).

Song actions can be found at *www.bigministries.co.uk*.

If you have time, you could also sing *Words Are Not Enough* (Track 6), which talks of worshipping God in more ways than just using our voices - perhaps with drums too!

 You will need:

10 mins

- Story script (starting on page 67)
- Rhythm instruments
- Red card
- Green card

Tell the children that whenever you hold up the green card they need to play a rhythm / sound that they think fits in with the story at that moment, and that you will help them with your arms like you did earlier.

Whenever you hold up the red card, there needs to be silence.

Practise this for a while!

 **EXPLORE THE BIBLE WITH RHYTHM**

4-7 mins

You will need:

- Bibles
- Rhythm instruments

Look up verses in the Bible that talk about using rhythm and music to praise God.

Perhaps read a verse aloud and invite the children to create some rhythmic sounds to worship God. You could even write a short song with them... perhaps bring in a guest from the music group in your church to help out!

Here's a few verses to get you started:

  - Psalm 33:3
  - Psalm 98
  - Psalm 150

 RHYTHM WORKSHOP [PART 2]

10 mins

You will need:

- Your drums or shaky eggs
- Everyone sitting in a circle
- A stop watch

1) *Pass the bang*

   Sitting on the floor in a circle, play a game of *Pass the Bang*. One person begins the game by facing either direction in the circle and banging their drum. The children then take it in turns to bang / shake their instrument until the noise has gone all the way round the circle.

   After a couple of practice runs, time it.

   Once the bang arrives back at the person who began, the timer must be stopped.

   Now try to beat your time. How fast can you *Pass the Bang*?

2) *What Does it Sound Like?*

   Start the game off by asking the children what an elephant sounds like and asking them to interpret what they think it sounds like on their instrument. Now ask them what a mouse sounds like and ask them to do the same. Next, go around the circle and ask each child to think of something different that everyone could interpret on their instrument. You don't need to stick to animals, it could be helicopters or thunder or trees; anything! Enjoy making loads of different noises to praise God.

PHILIP AND THE ETHIOPIAN OFFICIAL
(Acts 8:26-39)

Our story today is called, **[GREEN]** (drum role, please!) **[RED]**... Philip and the Ethiopian Official.

Philip was one of Jesus' followers and, even though Christians were being arrested and even killed at this time, Philip would still tell people about Jesus everywhere he went.

One day, Philip was visited by an angel.

"Philip," said the angel, "at noon today I want you to walk to that dusty desert road that goes from Jerusalem all the way down to Gaza."

There was no explanation as to why he was to go there, but Philip did as the angel requested and began a short walk to the dusty desert road...

[GREEN] Walking and walking and walking he went, at a fairly slow rhythmic pace. Walking and walking and walking he went, until eventually, Philip stopped! **[RED]**.

Philip was at the dusty desert road. The sun was high in the sky and Philip waited for only a short time before hearing a gentle rumbling sound that made the tiny stones and clumps of dust, on the dusty desert road, shake and bounce.

At first it was a gentle rumbling - ever so faint. **[GREEN]** So faint that you could only just about hear it if you listened carefully. Gradually, the rumbling grew a little louder... the dusty desert road began to shake a little more and a cloud of dust could be seen in the distance... a little louder and a little louder grew the rumbling sound. What was it? Who was it?... louder and louder grew the rumbling. It was now visible to Philip as to what the rumbling was. It was a chariot. The rumbling grew louder and louder and louder and louder and louder as the chariot sped past Philip! **[RED]**.

As the chariot sped past Philip, God prompted Philip to climb on board the chariot as it raced along the dusty desert road.

And so, Philip ran **[GREEN]** as fast as he could. He ran and ran and ran and eventually caught up with the chariot. Running alongside the chariot, Philip saw an Ethiopian official inside, whose job it was to look after all of the treasures of the Queen of Ethiopia. Philip could see that the Ethiopian was reading the book of Isaiah; reading some words that were written about Jesus.

"Do you understand what you're reading?" shouted Philip above all of the noise.

"Not really!" said the Ethiopian, "I need someone to explain it."

[RED] The chariot stopped, as did Philip.

Philip hopped on board and began to explain to the Ethiopian official all about Jesus, who He was, what He did, and how knowing Jesus could transform his life.

And so, with Philip still in the chariot, they set off. **[GREEN]**.

Slowly at first, with gentle rumbling, and then a little louder as they got faster and faster... and still, a little louder... and louder... and louder.... and faster and faster and faster until... **[RED]**...

"STOP!" cried the Ethiopian.

With that, the chariot screeched to a halt, its wheels skidding on the dusty desert road.

"Look," said the Ethiopian to Philip, "there's a stream of water just over there. How about you baptise me?"

And so, out of the chariot they hopped.

The Ethiopian stepped into the water, closely followed by Philip. Philip then baptised the Ethiopian official, but when he came up out of the water, Philip was nowhere to be seen. The Holy Spirit had taken Philip off to another place.

The Ethiopian didn't care though. He was so happy, that he hopped and skipped back into his chariot and praised God.

And then... the gentle rumbling began once again as the chariot set off...

[GREEN] It started very quietly as the wheels turned on the dusty desert road... and then gradually the rumbling of the wheels grew louder and louder and louder and louder. The chariot went off in to the distance, and as it did so, the noise on the dusty desert road gradually grew quieter and quieter and quieter until the chariot could not be heard at all. **[RED]**.

ABOUT US

BIG Ministries love to celebrate God and have loads of fun doing it! We mainly do this by putting on events across the country (check out the website to see if there are any near you) as well as writing resources for churches to use with their children's groups and in all-age services. You can even instantly download loads of interactive Bible stories from our website.

Get in touch if you think we could help you, or if you'd like to join us at an event!

t: 01527 556639
e: info@bigministries.co.uk
w: bigministries.co.uk

🐦 bigministriesuk
f bigministriesuk